INSPERIENCE THE DIVINE

Heart to Heart Conversations with the ONE

Gayatri Naraine and **Shireen Chada**

Published by Release Your Wings (www.releaseyourwings.net),
a Brahma Kumaris - USA (www.brahmakumaris.org/us) production.
tampa@us.brahmakumaris.org

ISBN 13 Paperback: 978-1-941883-02-0

For worldwide distribution. Printed in India.

Authors
Gayatri Naraine (Insperience meditations 1 through 33)
Shireen Chada (Insperience meditations 34 through 72)

Editors
H. D. Goswami
Leddy Hammock
Jane Kay
Karen Perusse
Karen Wesolowski

Design
Judi Rich

*To all those who have contributed to the making of **Insperience the Divine**—*
our heartfelt thanks.

This book is dedicated to Dadi Janki in honor of her 100th year.

Dadi, your life is a precious gift to all of us. You have nourished our hearts, grown our minds, and taught us to live beyond limits. Your footsteps have left a path for us to follow and we are determined to sustain your legacy of making the impossible possible.

Insperience and Other Key Terms Defined

In contrast to the word "experience"(literally, "*to perceive and feel what is outside ourselves*"), the new word "insperience" means, "*to perceive and feel what is within ourselves.*" In this book, insperience teaches us to see, recognize, and love the ONE. Hence we come to our definition:

Insperience *n*: To feel and understand the guidance, grace, and companionship of the ONE.

Let us define two more essential terms:

Drishti   Seeing, viewing, and beholding, especially with the mind's eye.

Karma Yoga   Action performed with consciousness connected to the ONE, or action and work in the world that connects to the ONE.

As a living being, the soul is most comfortable in a pure state of being. The soul seeks fulfillment and contentment in the domain of relationships. Harmonious relationships establish trust, worth, and dignity.

Being with ONE (an initiative of the Brahma Kumaris) gave individuals the opportunity to experience the pure joy of a relationship with the Source and to draw on the latent memories that live within the soul. We call the process of drawing upon these latent memories *insperience*. In contrast to ordinary *experience*, whose root meaning is to perceive and feel what is outside ourselves, the word *insperience* means to perceive and feel what is **within** ourselves.

This Being with ONE Initiative invited individuals into a daily, silent conversation. Content for *insperience* was offered as an entry point into conversation with the ONE. The content served to ignite subliminal memories and open the hearts full capacity for remembrance. The intention embedded in the *insperience* points allowed a natural, easy, and familiar flow of the souls relationship with the ONE. Our divine intellect, with divine insight, grasped these points.

Shireen Chada and I crafted the *insperience* points, through hours of studying the original teachings of the Brahma Kumaris Raja Yoga. Our founder, Prajapita Brahma, spoke to us these teachings, after first receiving them in his silent conversation with the ONE, who revealed to him profound spiritual truths. I wrote *insperience* pieces 1 to 33 and Shireen authored the pieces from 34 to 72.

We offered these *insperience* pieces over a period of 72 days, throughout the Being with ONE Initiative and they seemed to hit the target of what people yearn for, for themselves and their loved ones. We offer this book containing these precious pieces of *insperience* as sublime spiritual food for the soul.

Use these precious pieces of "*insperience*" to:

- immerse the self in silent conversation with the ONE;
- increase levels of fulfillment and contentment in relationship with the ONE as a foundation for relationships with others;
- inculcate the messages that manifest as guidelines for life;
- integrate being with doing and connect your soul to your role; and
- invoke joy in your journey of living, loving, learning, and laughing!

Gayatri Naraine

Table of Contents

Table of Contents

THE ONE

Introspection

Fulfilling the promise to the ONE.

Remembrance

Soul in Conversation with the ONE: My dear ONE, You are my ONE constant Companion, and my promise is that I am with You now, I will always stay with You, and I will return with You. It is when I stay connected to the ONE Source that I am able to fulfill my relationships with human beings.

The ONE in Conversation with the Soul: Sweet soul, the Bestower of Blessings loves the word, "one." Dear child, take strength from the ONE and support from the ONE. Together with this, follow the directions of the ONE. Experience the sweetness of the ONE. When the soul loves solitude, that is when you go into the depths of the ONE. You, too, will begin to love the word, "one."

Practice

Soul Conscious *Drishti*: The more I see others with love, the more my inner treasure of love increases. This is the service that I do. I radiate love with every glance in the remembrance of the ONE.

***Karma Yoga* Awareness:** I do not find anything difficult. In every thought, in every second, in every action, and in every step, I experience blessings and closeness and feel as if I am personally with the ONE.

THE DIVINE MOTHER

Introspection

Newness and divinity are the special supports of life.

Remembrance

Soul in Conversation with the ONE: My dear ONE, You made me a trustee of my thoughts, time, and resources. You asked me to consider how long I engage in ordinary thoughts, words, and actions; and how long they are divine and elevated.

The ONE in Conversation with the Soul: Sweet soul, the Mother decorates the child with divinity and says: Dear child, as your Mother, I nurture you with divine life, divine intellect, divine words, and divine actions, so that you can know the difference between ordinary and divine existence.

Practice

Soul Conscious *Drishti*: A soul who lives a divine life gives others the experience of divinity through his/her divine eyes, taking them, with just one glance beyond the ordinary state into the original divine self.

Karma Yoga **Awareness:** Throughout the day, I gave no one sorrow. This was ordinary. But did I give anyone happiness? This is divine. Today, I did not waste my thoughts. This is ordinary. But did I use my thoughts in creative, beneficial ways? This is divine.

DILARAM: THE COMFORTER OF HEARTS

Introspection

The sound of a true heart attracts many others to the Comforter of Hearts.

Remembrance

Soul in Conversation with the ONE: My dear ONE, You always tell me to remember You with a true heart. You never say to remember You with a true head. You say that the Lord is pleased with the one who has a true heart. You do not say that the Lord is pleased with the one who has a clever head.

The ONE in Conversation with the Soul: Sweet soul, human life rests on head and heart. The head should be wise and the heart should be true. The ONE lays the hand of blessings on the head of those with a true heart, for He is the Comforter of Hearts. You receive subtle inspirations, full of significance for thoughts, words, and actions when your head is wise and the heart is true.

Practice

Soul Conscious *Drishti:* When I contemplate on how well I am progressing, my vision focuses only on the ONE, and the self. I see the me I want to be. When others see the change in me, they are transformed.

***Karma Yoga* Awareness:** Do I move forward based on an honest heart or am I only trapped in simply intellectualizing? If I only intellectualize, then when I speak to others, only their intellect will be affected; whereas if I speak from the heart, what I say will touch the hearts of others.

THE MASTER OF THE TREE

Introspection

Souls are sparkling stars decorating the *Kalpa* (genealogical) Tree of humanity. Each star shines in a special way.

Remembrance

Soul in Conversation with the ONE: My dear ONE, as a soul on the tree of souls, I receive sustenance directly from the Master Seed and I become powerful. This direct link to the Powerhouse ensures that I never become depleted, and just as stars in the sky simply shine, I do not need to compete with the light of others.

The ONE in Conversation with the Soul: Sweet soul, you live on the tree of souls with a direct link to the Supreme Soul, the ONE Master. You say with experience and rapture that the ONE is the Mother and Father who created you. Remember the wonderful uniqueness of this great relationship.

Practice

Soul Conscious *Drishti*: In the same way as I appreciate the unique qualities of others, I recognise my own and use them to link to others. In this way, my good qualities multiply.

***Karma Yoga* Awareness:** I put this sustenance into practice by using the spiritual powers in the right situation and place at the time of need.

THE UNLIMITED

Introspection

The Unlimited ONE gives unlimited gifts.

Remembrance

Soul in Conversation with the ONE: My dear ONE, You brought heaven on the palm of Your hand and placed it gently in my own. Those who accept this greatest gift become the most elevated human beings.

The ONE in Conversation with the Soul: Sweet soul, in this greatest age, the unlimited ONE gives you the greatest gift: the fortune of paradise on earth. The gifts of even the most important human beings are like lamps next to the Sun, compared with this gift of the ONE.

Practice

Soul Conscious *Drishti*: Through my eyes, endless waves of spiritual fulfilment, of peace and happiness—reach other souls.

***Karma Yoga* Awareness:** My inheritance is full and unlimited. I live in deep contentment with my actions and relationships.

POINT OF LIGHT

Introspection

In my heart, I constantly envision the ONE as the incorporeal light.

Remembrance

Soul in Conversation with the ONE: My dear ONE, across the world, people have tried to remember You by portraying You in various memorials. Now, with wonder, I come to know You as You really are. Now I can actually meet You and I celebrate!

The ONE in Conversation with the Soul: Sweet soul, delight in the knowledge that I made you powerful, with no limit to your light. You are My child, and as I am a Point of Light, so you are also a point of light. Love emerges as soon as you experience yourself as My child. This is a living awareness. As a tree lives in a seed, so all wisdom lives in the all-knowing ONE.

Practice

Soul Conscious *Drishti*: Recognizing the great fortune that shines through a point of light in the center of my forehead, I see my world differently.

***Karma Yoga* Awareness:** Detachment brings easy success in every action. While listening and speaking to others, I focus on the soul as a point of light, fixed in this awareness. My powerful detachment and love flow into the world.

THE LAWMAKER

Introspection

The True Guide is the ONE who makes your thoughts, words, and actions truthful and aligns you with the laws of life.

Remembrance

Soul in Conversation with the ONE: My dear ONE, beyond human-made laws and disciplines, there are spiritual laws and disciplines. As the ONE True Guide, You help me see the difference and follow the higher principles. When I do, You call me a lawmaker.

The ONE in Conversation with the Soul: Sweet soul, until there is balance between love and law, you are not a lawmaker. One who forgets the soul and makes the body all, breaks the law. To keep yourself constantly within the law, you must now focus on the soul. Then you will never be defeated. If you wish to be a lawmaker, do not break this law. Do not lose yourself in the machine of the body; see the life of the body, which is the soul.

Practice

Soul Conscious *Drishti:* Living as a soul, and so staying within the law, I destroy evil with a glance.

***Karma Yoga* Awareness:** I take my steps with careful thought and consideration. I conduct myself according to the law.

THE OCEAN OF LOVE

Introspection

You are the Ocean of Love, and we, Your children, claim Your love as an inheritance.

Remembrance

Soul in Conversation with the ONE: My dear ONE, as the Ocean of Love, You come to meet us. Your unlimited love gives us courage to be our true self. Your love easily makes us forget the past. Your love sustains and strengthens us to continue on the pilgrimage of remembrance.

The ONE in Conversation with the Soul: Sweet soul, all souls are equal in the eyes of the ONE. All souls are seen and treated as loving. The ONE is like an Ocean—giving generously and constantly. Souls who always love receive love easily for they are above obstacles and difficulties. They have a right to all powers and victories. The ONE becomes their world and only the ONE is the source of their love.

Practice

Soul Conscious *Drishti:* Balancing on the waves of love, my eyes behold the horizon. There I see new hope and possibilities.

***Karma Yoga* Awareness:** I act like a lotus—detached from stress and difficulty with deep love for the ONE.

THE GARDENER

Introspection

The Spiritual Gardener is beholding his garden of spiritual roses and enjoying the splendour of the beauty of those in full bloom, the sweetness of those in bud, and the fragrance of virtues radiating in all directions.

Remembrance

Soul in Conversation with the ONE: My dear ONE, the flowers love the Master of the Garden and the Master of the Garden loves the flowers. However, all the flowers are not the same. Some have the fragrance of knowledge, some the fragrance of remembrance, some of *dharna,* and some of service. Some are complete with all fragrance. So where is Your vision drawn first?

The ONE in Conversation with the Soul: Sweet soul, all the spiritual roses grow in the garden of the Spiritual Gardener. The Gardener's gaze falls on all the roses and appreciates the fragrance, color, beauty, and bloom of each one. Within each rose there is intense love for the ONE Gardener. Every day the ONE Gardener celebrates his encounter with all the roses and nurtures them with love and care.

Practice

Soul Conscious *Drishti:* My eyes will look for the special virtue in every flower and offer it to the Gardener.

***Karma Yoga* Awareness:** I feel so much gratitude toward the ONE Gardener. As I witness the actions of others, I will remember to thank the Gardener for what I learn from the beauty and fragrance of the many flowers in His garden.

THE SEED

Introspection

Embedded in the Seed are the secrets of the tree.

Remembrance

Soul in Conversation with the ONE: My dear ONE, as the Seed of the world tree, You sow in us knowledge that we are master seeds. You join us to the field of thought and teach us to purify the mind, and remove the weeds. You connect us to the field of feelings and show us how to become new saplings.

The ONE in Conversation with the Soul: Sweet soul, the Seed of the tree is seeing the children who are the foundation of the new tree, those who are taking sustenance from the Seed of the tree. The Seed is revealing the secrets of the 3 aspects of time—past, present, and future; the secrets of the 3 dimensions—incorporeal, subtle, and corporeal; and the secrets of the 3 divine acts of the ONE creation, sustenance, and transformation. These secrets reveal to the souls the highest form of service called *mansa seva.*

Practice

Soul Conscious *Drishti:* I use the third eye to see the subtle flow of elevated thoughts taking shape in the golden field of my mind.

***Karma Yoga* Awareness:** Cooperation is when I connect the seed of thoughts to actions that create a greater good.

THE PURIFIER

Introspection

A pure life is a blessing bestowed by The ONE.

Remembrance

Soul in Conversation with the ONE: My dear ONE, with the power of knowledge I have understood that the original, eternal form of the "I," the soul, is pure. Once I recollected this and strengthened this awareness, purity became a living reality. Purity is not just abstinence from sinful actions; it is intrinsic to the soul. Purity is foundational to the fortune of many lifetimes.

The ONE in Conversation with the Soul: Sweet soul, the ONE Mother and Father give the blessing of purity at the moment of each child's spiritual birth. Purity is a canopy that shields us from the innumerable obstacles of *Maya*. Purity is the foundation of peace and happiness. The ONE Purifier purifies the souls with yoga-fire. This power of purity, over time, restores the soul to its original and complete form of light.

Practice

Soul Conscious *Drishti*: With spiritual purity, the eyes are always clean and pure. Their sparkle transforms others into embodiments of sparkling lights.

***Karma Yoga* Awareness:** Respecting my self, I keep my temple, the body, always clean and in simplicity. The ONE entrusted this temple to me. Purity in body will constantly bring spiritual happiness.

THE POET

Introspection

The Poet renders in words a perfect portrait of fortune.

Remembrance

Soul in Conversation with the ONE: My dear ONE, to express the fortune that You narrated to me is to apply it in my life. You, the Maker of Fortune, distribute fortune to everyone. Because each expresses their fortune differently —whether in paintings or in poems—fortune is unique to each one. The ONE has given us talent and tools to be our own poets and to paint our own portraits.

The ONE in Conversation with the Soul: Sweet soul, your portrait of fortune has a unique splendor. The specialness of your fortune shines in your eyes and smile. Your eyes, your spiritual *drishti*, are filled with innocence, mercy, and benevolence. The splendor of contentment and cheerfulness put a spiritual glow on your face in the form of a smile. Now all that remains are the final touches of perfection and completion.

Practice

Soul Conscious *Drishti*: Am I happy seeing others move forward? I am, but I should not remain behind. I must see them alongside me. With benevolent eyes, I must move forward and encourage those behind me to move beside me.

Karma Yoga **Awareness:** My actions are the pen that writes my poetic acts. Poetic acts liberate me from the constraints of life and free me to paint my portrait on the canvas of life.

THE OCEAN OF BLISS

Introspection

Balance is bliss.

Remembrance

Soul in Conversation with the ONE: My dear ONE, I walk the tightrope of life and the wonder is in keeping my balance. When I hear praise, I become intoxicated. When I hear defamation, I become upset. So, what should I do? I should neither be intoxicated with praise nor upset with defamation! I should be a detached observer and experience wonders. I should feel content inside. When I lack this effort, I do not have a blissful life.

The ONE in Conversation with the Soul: Sweet soul, when you are equal in praise and defamation, victory and defeat, happiness and sorrow, you are balanced to be equal in dualities as equanimity. Without equanimity, you are imbalanced and cannot experience bliss from the ONE. If you wish to experience bliss from the ONE, always maintain a balance of love and power.

Practice

Soul Conscious *Drishti*: When the balance is off and I watch the games of fluctuation as a detached observer, I find it very humorous. In the same way, I must look at my own self when *Maya* makes me a little unconscious, or when she makes me lose the awareness of my elevated stage. If I look at myself as a detached observer, I will be able to adjust the balance.

Karma Yoga Awareness: I should perform action (karma) with virtuous principles (*dharma*). When I balance karma and *dharma*, my impact grows.

THE OCEAN OF PEACE

Introspection

By using the water of powerful remembrance, you can experience immediate peace.

Remembrance

Soul in Conversation with the ONE: My dear ONE, we say, "*Om shanti*" three times—the first is to remember that the ONE is the Source of peace, the second is to connect to the *swadharma* (religion of the soul) as peace, and the third is to return to the Home, the silent abode of peace.

The ONE in Conversation with the Soul: Sweet soul, the Home of souls is the silent world of peace. When souls return to their Home, they are nurtured by silence in their eternal seed stage of peace. Peace connects the soul to its home, to the Source, and to its sovereignty. When souls (who love peace) experience pure peace, they are drawn to that pure peace again and again.

Practice

Soul Conscious *Drishti*: As a master bestower of peace, my powerful, pure feelings will shine through my eyes and naturally inspire elevated pure feelings of peace in others.

***Karma Yoga* Awareness:** With the practice of the power of silence, my actions will flourish in the energy field of peace.

NIRAKARI: INCORPOREAL

Introspection

I, beyond the material body, use the body, and I speak.

Remembrance

Soul in Conversation with the ONE: My dear ONE, You asked me, "Who are you? Are you the body, or something beyond it?" Then You said, "You are beyond the body! Why do you forget this? Do not forget your original form, beyond matter, and remember that the material body is your instrument."

The ONE in Conversation with the Soul: Sweet soul, the ONE enters the stage of sound from the stage beyond sound to give His children the experience of life beyond matter. The Incorporeal ONE communicates through sound yet remains aware of existing beyond sound. The *Shivalingam* represents the ONE beyond matter, and the *saligrams* represent the souls beyond matter.

Practice

Soul Conscious *Drishti*: When I stabilize myself in the incorporeal consciousness, then I am able to see the wonders of the ONE.

***Karma Yoga* Awareness:** I embody this mantra: "I am pure soul living in matter." With this awareness, I act as a pure soul beyond matter.

THE BOATMAN

Introspection

Wise is the one who surrenders his/her boat to the ONE, knowing the destiny of the destination is fixed.

Remembrance

Soul in Conversation with the ONE: My dear ONE, it feels like all human beings are sitting in a boat, sailing in turbulent waters, and the rising tides are causing the boat to rock. The burden of the collective sins is sinking the boat. Not knowing what else to do, we call out, "Oh, Boatman! Take our boat across. Lead us safely to our destination!"

The ONE in Conversation with the Soul: Sweet soul, the company of the ONE is the company of the Truth. When you are in the company of the Truth, you are safe. Nothing from the outside can shake you, you will stay unshakeable. When the boat and the Boatman are strong, then storms become a means to make the boat move forward. The boat of truth may shake, but it will never sink. Place the hand of your intellect into the hand of the Boatman. He will calm the waters and lead you to your destination.

Practice

Soul Conscious *Drishti*: When my two eyes are focused on the Lighthouse and my third eye is in the company of the Truth, the tidal waves of fear subside.

***Karma Yoga* Awareness:** When I do actions while seated in the boat of truth, each physical organ is aligned to spiritual order.

AJANMA: BEYOND BIRTH & DEATH

Introspection

There is only ONE who remains beyond birth and death.

Remembrance

Soul in Conversation with the ONE: My dear ONE, You teach me how to live and You teach me how to die alive. You lit the path of the soul's transition from one body to another distinguishing the soul from the Supreme Soul.

The ONE in Conversation with the Soul: Sweet soul, only the ONE Supreme Soul, the Almighty, the Ever-free ONE, the Purifier, the ONE who never performs wrong actions (*Vikarmajit*), the ONE who is beyond the fruits of actions (*Karmateet*), the ONE who is beyond thoughts (*Asochota*), the ONE who is beyond desires (*Abhogta*), the ONE who is beyond divine virtues and beyond devilish traits, the ONE who always resides in the land beyond sound but is called the Creator of heaven on earth, the ONE who knows the three aspects of time, but is never influenced by time, only that ONE is beyond birth and death.

Practice

Soul Conscious *Drishti*: Only the third eye can understand the mystery of who takes birth, who dies, and who remains beyond.

***Karma Yoga* Awareness:** When I am caught in the bog of my karmic accounts of my many births, I reach out to the ONE who is ever-pure and beyond the law of karma.

THE ALCHEMIST

Introspection

The "Intellect of the Wise" changes a stone-like intellect into a golden vessel.

Remembrance

Soul in Conversation with the ONE: My dear ONE, there is significance to the dot which is placed on the memorial image of the *Shivalingam*. Then there are three drops of water that are sprinkled on the image. Is there a connection of this ritual to the method of making the intellect golden?

The ONE in Conversation with the Soul: Sweet soul, this process is connected to the method used in remembrance of the ONE: the dot is the image of the Source and the drops are elevated thoughts that the soul creates of itself. The first drop is "I am a soul." The second drop is "I am a child of the Supreme Soul." The third drop is "I am a trustee of my body, mind, and wealth." The pure energy of these elevated thoughts comes directly from the Source and transforms the intellect, drop by drop. The intellect is transformed from stone into gold, from ignorance into enlightenment, and becomes the golden instrument to pioneer the path of truth.

Practice

Soul Conscious *Drishti*: I see enlightenment with the vessel of my golden intellect.

***Karma Yoga* Awareness:** My actions are nourished by the sweet drops of the highest knowledge dripping into my intellect.

THE TRAVELER

Introspection

Traveling with the Companion.

Remembrance

Soul in Conversation with the ONE: My dear ONE, I am a traveler of life. I have been stumbling over the potholes of "why," "what," "who," "how," and "where." I have become very tired wandering around seeking the ONE. The path has become difficult, the footsteps heavy, and the heart has shrunk and has lost hope. The traveler needs a companion.

The ONE in Conversation with the Soul: Sweet soul, companions are those who stay together and travel together, side by side, step by step and experience the path to be easy, clear, and accurate. Every step taken with the elevated Companion makes the path clear and clean. All you have to do is keep your steps aligned with the Companion's steps and move forward. The Companion knows all the solutions. So move in whatever direction the Companion takes.

Practice

Soul Conscious *Drishti:* In a pure state of mind, my spiritual eyes show me the path on the journey of life.

***Karma Yoga* Awareness:** Before I act, I must verify my thought to make sure that it is aligned to that of my Companion.

THE PROTECTOR

Introspection

Remain in the furnace of powerful remembrance of the ONE and be protected from an environment of fear and worry.

Remembrance

Soul in Conversation with the ONE: My dear ONE, the one desire of most souls is to experience real, true safety. Is it possible to feel safe in today's world? Is it possible to protect the self from the uncertain realities that exist? Can there be ONE canopy under which all souls can return to protect their hearts from sorrow and pain and their lives from doubts and fears, and to reclaim the specialties of peace and love?

The ONE in Conversation with the Soul: Sweet soul, the canopy of protection is a sacred, safe, and secure space in which the soul receives spiritual power and peace. The method of protection from the force of destruction is the power of fearlessness. Such a critical time is to come in which the power of remembrance of the ONE will become the means of safety like an armor around you. In advance of this time, create an atmosphere of powerful remembrance in which you will be safe and will be able to give the cooperation of your own peace and power to other souls so that they too feel safe. This is the ONE canopy.

Practice

Soul Conscious *Drishti*: An honest heart protects my eyes from being deceived by the realities of uncertainty.

***Karma Yoga* Awareness:** Under the canopy of protection, I am able to hear the call of time.

THE ONE WHO FORGIVES

Introspection

The nature of the ONE is forgiveness.

Remembrance

Soul in Conversation with the ONE: My dear ONE, I make a lot of effort to correct myself and others, but I do not know how to forgive. You told me that no matter how angry someone may get, do not absorb their anger and harbor resentment. Anger and resentment are blocks to forgiveness.

The ONE in Conversation with the Soul: Sweet soul, you come in front of the ONE and say, "Give me blessings, have mercy on me, forgive me." Once blessings and mercy are received from the ONE, use them to cool the inner resentment, anger, and distrust that you carry. Do not seek revenge, but clean the self and set it free with truth. Forgiveness is to change the awareness with understanding and to use the virtues of the soul as healing energies.

Practice

Soul Conscious *Drishti:* With a sweet vision and clean attitude I can let go in one minute every block to forgiveness.

***Karma Yoga* Awareness:** When I pave my path with spiritual sense, then every step will put me on the higher ground of forgiveness.

SATYAM SHIVAM SUNDARAM: THE TRUTH, BENEVOLENT, BEAUTIFUL

Introspection

True Benevolent Beauty

Remembrance

Soul in Conversation with the ONE: My dear ONE, Your true benevolent beauty has been written about in poetry, lyrics, movie scripts, teaching texts, and love letters. The *"insperience"* is: "Your touch of truth is like raindrops of rose water. Your warm benevolence is like the brilliance of a thousand suns. Your majestic beauty is like heaven—your perfect replication."

The ONE in Conversation with the Soul: Sweet soul, I am the ONE who is the embodiment of truth. I am *Satyam*. I am the ONE whose heart is overflowing with benevolence. I am *Shivam*. I am the ONE whose beauty is indescribable. I am *Sundaram*.

Practice

Soul Conscious *Drishti:* It is the eye of *"insperience"* that knows and recognizes the ONE.

***Karma Yoga* Awareness:** The soul receives the pen of karma to write its story of fortune with the signature of truth, benevolence, and beauty.

PANDAVPATI: THE LORD OF THE PANDAVAS

Introspection

The Pandava army stands on the Ocean shore in the company of the ONE. (The five Pandava brothers fought heroically for justice in a troubled ancient world.)

Remembrance

Soul in Conversation with the ONE: My dear ONE, I should remember that the Pandavas were always victorious because they chose the ONE. However it seems that today, even the most faithful fluctuate between victory and defeat. What is missing in our efforts?

The ONE in Conversation with the Soul: Sweet soul, when you forget your gifts and instead look at other objects, then you are defeated. Remember your gift and you will be victorious. Believe in one another and you will change the motives and intentions of others. Your faith will cleanse people's motives. You will inspire new intentions in them. Although each Pandava was a strong, unique warrior, they put aside their selfish motives and fought together for victory. This unity was their special gift. They acted with one feeling and one wish in their love for ONE. This always brought them victory.

Practice

Soul Conscious *Drishti*: When I see something that is not right, I do not allow it to fester in my heart, for that would blur my own vision.

***Karma Yoga* Awareness:** When I truly listen to others, I am able to uplift and transform their meaning and engage them in beneficial actions. Otherwise, I hear without truly listening.

THE WIZARD'S KEY

Introspection

I have total rights to the ONE's treasures.

Remembrance

Soul in Conversation with the ONE: My dear ONE, You have handed us the secrets of all of Your treasures. But have we become knowledgeable and sensible in looking after this key? Do we know how to use this key to attain whatever we want in a second?

The ONE in Conversation with the Soul: Sweet soul, to belong to the ONE and to remember the ONE is the method to use the key. The key has the potion to make you into the embodiment of any power, as soon as you invoke it. Become the resident of any of the three dimensions in a second: silence, thought, and sound. Be in any of the three aspects of time: past, present, future. Reclaim the right over the power of thought and direct these aspects of time into whatever direction you choose.

Practice

Soul Conscious *Drishti:* I keep my eye on the key at all times.

***Karma Yoga* Awareness:** Before I begin any task, I will use the key to invoke the power that is needed for success.

THE JEWELER

Introspection

You are the jewels of the eyes.

Remembrance

Soul in Conversation with the ONE: My dear ONE, the nine jewels are remembered as the souls who have destroyed all variety of obstacles. Devotees keep different forms of the nine jewels to remove obstacles from their path. What is the specialty of such jewels?

The ONE in Conversation with the Soul: Sweet soul, you are sitting in a unique court of invaluable jewels, Godly jewels. The value of you, the Godly jewels, the children of the ONE, is the most elevated of all. Each jewel is said to have its own specialty and is praised as a destroyer of particular obstacles. Whether or not you, yourself, realize your own value, the ONE has seen the worthiness of you and has given you the key to His treasure chest. You are master mines of the jewels of knowledge. The more you use your jewels, the more they increase.

Practice

Soul Conscious *Drishti*: When I, the soul, look through my eyes into the eyes of another, I see the jewel of the soul shining back at me. This is spiritual vision.

***Karma Yoga* Awareness:** My specialties are like precious gems. Each specialty reflects newness in my actions. And my words are like pearls.

THE MESSENGER

Introspection

The final message is: "This is the ONE." Experience a whole new world within ONE.

Remembrance

Soul in Conversation with the ONE: My dear ONE, Your message is clear and simple: All human beings are souls, all souls are brothers and sisters, and as souls we have ONE Mother and Father. Your mission is to thread us all into the rosary of victory.

The ONE in Conversation with the Soul: Sweet soul, I am the Messenger and you are living the message. You inculcate My teachings and turn them into principles. You follow My directions and make them into specialties. You become the message and reveal the Messenger.

Practice

Soul Conscious *Drishti:* In being the message others see the liberation.

***Karma Yoga* Awareness:** In living the message, I walk my talk.

JADUGAR: THE MAGICIAN

Introspection

Making the impossible into the possible with the magic mantra.

Remembrance

Soul in Conversation with the ONE: My dear ONE, I have become very experienced with words. If I do not get the opportunity to serve through words, I feel empty and bored. I keep planning programs, organizing conferences and get-togethers. Then, it seems that service is beginning to lose its magic. What is the new wave of service that will show wonders and drum rolls of magic?

The ONE in Conversation with the Soul: Sweet soul, the majority is comfortable moving forward with the enthusiasm of words. Now, the new wave of serving needs to be with the mind: *mansa seva*, serving through the mind, is the new specialty that is needed now to show wonders. The practice of *mansa seva* becomes magic. Use the magic mantra and bring about newness. Let there be the meeting of the mind and words. Develop pure feelings and good wishes in the mind. The balance of the two is the magic mantra. The magic mantra changes thoughts, feelings, and words into blessings.

Practice

Soul Conscious *Drishti*: When the intellect is connected to the ONE, the vibrations that radiate from the eyes have magical powers.

***Karma Yoga* Awareness:** With a divine intellect, experience the magic touching from the ONE and success will flow from every action.

KHUDA DOST: THE FRIEND

Introspection

Listen to the call of your number ONE Friend.

Remembrance

Soul in Conversation with the ONE: My dear ONE, only You are my love, only You are my friend, my Beloved. I speak to only You, listen to only You. I only want to dance with You. That is bliss. If you want to know about supreme bliss, ask the friends of the ONE.

The ONE in Conversation with the Soul: Sweet soul, who else would have so many true spiritual friends? No one else but the ONE has or will have so many close friends. A friend means someone who is always kept close. To have a friend means that you are never alone. Whether you are called children or friends, all of you say with a right to the ONE: "You are mine!" And *Khuda Dhost* says to each one: "You are Mine! Oh My wonderful friends!" The Friend of the heart sings the song of the specialty of each spiritual friend. He is telling the secrets of His heart to the friends of His Heart.

Practice

Soul Conscious *Drishti*: When I am able to see my enemy as a friend, I am able to separate the pearl of insight from the stone of blindness.

Karma Yoga **Awareness:** I walk with my Friend in perfect harmony.

SAT CHIT ANANDA: TRUTH, LIVING, BLISSFUL

Introspection

The most glorious ONE's form is: truth, living, and blissful.

Remembrance

Soul in Conversation with the ONE: My dear ONE, Your praises are sung in remembrance of the truth You revealed. The glory of Your divine acts are living in the memorials people created. Your blessings are forever cherished as blissful memories.

The ONE in Conversation with the Soul: Sweet soul, You embody the qualities with which to glorify the ONE. Through your mouth, let only words of truth be spoken. Let your face reflect the specialties of divinity. Let the sparkle of bliss shine through the living soul from the center of the forehead.

Practice

Soul Conscious *Drishti*: What vision will someone have through my eyes? Whatever is in my attitude will be seen through my eyes.

***Karma Yoga* Awareness:** When my outer action is connected to an inner intention of truth, it leaves a blissful trail of living vibrations.

THE ALL-EMBRACING ONE

Introspection

The ONE belongs to all.

Remembrance

Soul in Conversation with the ONE: My dear ONE, Your arms are so big and Your heart so generous that You are able to hold everyone in a warm, tender, and loving embrace. In Your embrace there is safety, security, and surety. In Your heart there is equality, ecstasy, and exuberance.

The ONE in Conversation with the Soul: Sweet soul, I embrace each soul as My "long-lost, now found child." In My embrace, each child reclaims the right to sit on the throne of My heart. In My heart, each soul is an invaluable jewel who embraces life with honesty and cleanliness. The Lord is pleased with honest hearts.

Practice

Soul Conscious *Drishti*: When my eyes remain cool and spiritual, I am able to take others beyond all differences with just one glance.

***Karma Yoga* Awareness:** In remembrance of ONE, I am able to act with the unifying principle that we are all one family.

THE MAJESTIC ONE

Introspection

The majestic Director makes an entrance on the world drama stage.

Remembrance

Soul in Conversation with the ONE: My dear ONE, when You made Your majestic entrance onto the world drama stage, You reminded us that we are all actors and not mere spectators. We are heroes and heroines and the eyes of the world are focused on the parts we are playing. The script of our roles is in the hands of You, the Director.

The ONE in Conversation with the Soul: Sweet soul, I am the ONE who is most loved in the world. I narrate the story of immortality, the story of the third eye, and the story of becoming a true deity to you, personally. These stories reach deep down into your memory bank and emerge your true, authentic self. I restore each child to the majesty of the soul's original sovereignty.

Practice

Soul Conscious *Drishti*: My eyes possess a certain majesty.

***Karma Yoga* Awareness:** Spiritual actions will give others the inspiration to become spiritual.

THE NOBLE ONE

Introspection

The ONE wins my heart with nobility.

Remembrance

Soul in Conversation with the ONE: My dear ONE, when no one else understood me, when everything I did went wrong, You gave me hope and understanding, and the strength to carry on. With nobility You won my heart. Your simple words were like arrows that pierced the core of my being, and truth, like a fountain, began to flow with gentility and grace. I was raised to a magnitude of royal dimensions.

The ONE in Conversation with the Soul: Sweet soul, your original state is one of nobility in character, of royal ancestry. You belong to the divine community of gods and goddesses. I color you with My company and the memory of divinity returns. I decorate you with jewels of knowledge and the crown of enlightenment takes form. I purify you with the fire of love and make you into a master of almighty authority.

Practice

Soul Conscious *Drishti:* The graciousness in my eyes reveals the nobility in my character.

***Karma Yoga* Awareness:** Nobility in actions is: less is more.

THE BESTOWER OF HONOR

Introspection

You changed me from a thorn into a flower and I began to bloom.

Remembrance

Soul in Conversation with the ONE: My dear ONE, You changed my form and fragrance, and made me into an honorable being. Realizing my true form, I regained self-respect, exuding the celestial fragrance of divine virtues, reflecting the clear colors of light, and appreciating my own spiritual beauty.

The ONE in Conversation with the Soul: Sweet soul, your highest honor is to realize your original, eternal identity. You are an eternal seed, a soul with unlimited potential. Originally you are a celestial flower of indescribable beauty. Use your unlimited potential, strive with determination, and you will complete yourself. You awake your indescribable beauty by aspiring to excellence in the arts of life.

Practice

Soul Conscious *Drishti*: *"Beauty is in the eye of the beholder."*

***Karma Yoga* Awareness:** My awareness is the soil, my thought is the seed, and my action is the fruit.

BHAGYA VIDHATA: THE BESTOWER OF FORTUNE

Introspection

The fruit of a thousand elevated thoughts is received from the ONE in return for one elevated thought of the soul.

Remembrance

Soul in Conversation with the ONE: My dear ONE, You give me multi-million times more than even what my mind can comprehend. You give me the key to attain complete happiness, peace, and power. You give all treasures equally to everyone at the same time. All I need is an honest heart and a clean heart. When instead of contemplating about my eternal self, I start thinking about others; and when instead of transforming myself, I want to change others, then I receive only a drop.

The ONE in Conversation with the Soul: Sweet soul, the ONE has given you the greatest of all treasures. This is the treasure of elevated thoughts—thoughts filled with good wishes and pure feelings. The ONE has shown you the way to make your fortune elevated. You do this by performing elevated actions. The basis of elevated actions is to have an elevated awareness. To remain aware of the ONE means to perform elevated actions.

Practice

Soul Conscious *Drishti*: I keep my vision clean, clear, and focused on the ONE.

***Karma Yoga* Awareness:** The task of world service is guaranteed to be successful. The ONE becomes an instrument to give a return of multi-millions for one. Therefore, I give voluntarily and with determination.

THE CLEVER ENTERTAINER

Introspection

Does the ONE ever have a desire?

Remembrance

Soul in Conversation with the ONE: My dear ONE, You are so entertaining and attractive. Because, You, the Creator, are entertaining, Your creation, the residents of the Golden Age and the Golden Age, is also entertaining. You have the attraction of purity. Because You are so pure, I am beginning to realize that You are free from desires and so why did You have the desire to come meet me?

The ONE in Conversation with the Soul: Sweet soul, yes, I have a desire; I have a desire to fulfill your pure desires. I am called the Clever Entertainer and I have to fulfill your desires in an entertaining way. Sometimes, I use my own discretion to fulfill your desires. Why do I fulfill your desires? Because you are the light of My eyes.

Practice

Soul Conscious *Drishti*: I see through the eyes of the ONE. I observe the Drama as drama. I become a witness and feel entertained by the Drama as it unfolds in my life.

***Karma Yoga* Awareness:** I maintain a balance between being entertaining and serious.

THE SUPREME FATHER

Introspection

The ONE is the loveliest Father of all. I, His child, always have the ONE's blessings.

Remembrance

Soul in Conversation with the ONE: My dear ONE, You are the Ocean of Love and that is why everyone calls You the Father. I understand that the Supreme Father means the Father of souls. I, the soul have the intoxication of being adopted by You, because, I receive Your full inheritance.

The ONE in Conversation with the Soul: Sweet soul, whatever you are, as you are, the ONE Father loves you. The first thing the Father does is to bring you into a lovely relationship of the family of the ONE. The ONE loves every child equally. No one should think that, "This one is loved more and I am loved less." The ONE, the Supreme Father, has two concerns: To educate you children and then make you into the heirs of the Golden Age.

Practice

Soul Conscious *Drishti:* When I see the ONE, I experience great happiness, because, I am the child of the ONE.

***Karma Yoga* Awareness:** I have the pure pride of being engaged in the ONE Father's business of transforming the world.

THE OCEAN OF PURITY

Introspection

The ONE is first of all the Ocean of Purity.

Remembrance

Soul in Conversation with the ONE: My dear ONE, You are the Ocean of Purity—Your innocence is like a newborn baby. None of the vices even touch Your thoughts. Your greatness is defined by Your personality of purity. You are altruistic and are constantly serving because of Your royalty of purity.

The ONE in Conversation with the Soul: Sweet soul, recognize and accept yourself as a pure soul and belong to the ONE. This faith is the basis of your purity. The ONE is the Ocean of Knowledge and hence the Ocean of Purity. Fill your intellects with thoughts of your original and eternal form and you will experience the ONE as the sweet Ocean of Purity.

Practice

Soul Conscious *Drishti:* I become a point and apply a full stop and focus on the Ocean of Purity.

***Karma Yoga* Awareness:** I renounce the arrogance of wanting to be consulted and the feeling of being insulted.

THE REMOVER OF SORROW & BESTOWER OF HAPPINESS

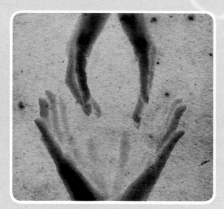

Introspection

The ONE has to make souls happy because the ONE is happy in the happiness of the souls.

Remembrance

Soul in Conversation with the ONE: My dear ONE, You saw the sorrow I was carrying. You have especially come to give me infinite happiness. You remove my sorrow without absorbing it Yourself. You are happy when I am happy. Although Your happiness never fluctuates, You cannot tolerate my sorrow.

I used to remember You only when I was in sorrow, but now I welcome You as my Companion in all the happy moments.

The ONE in Conversation with the Soul: Sweet soul, I don't give you sorrow, you receive sorrow from your own actions. I am removing the shadows that have kept you afraid and in the dark. I cannot bear to see you confused or stumbling, because you are more loved than life.

Practice

Soul Conscious *Drishti:* The ONE, the Bestower of Happiness, sees me dancing in the waves of super sensuous joy.

***Karma Yoga* Awareness:** I experience the gift of happiness as a reminder of my perfect stage and my future Golden Aged life.

THE SUN OF KNOWLEDGE

Introspection

I withdraw my attention from the world outside and center myself on the seat of the soul.

Remembrance

Soul in Conversation with the ONE: My dear ONE, You play such an important role in my life. Your teachings have helped me dispel the darkness of ignorance. Without Your wisdom I wouldn't have a spiritual life. My spiritual growth is because of the light of Your wisdom. Daily exposure to the light of Your wisdom is making me divine.

The ONE in Conversation with the Soul: Sweet soul, you are so precious that I had to come to you personally and illuminate your beauty. Shining the light of knowledge will dispel doubts and will brighten the darkest corners of the soul.

Practice

Soul Conscious *Drishti:* I look at souls and have the pure thought: May the Sun of Knowledge rise in their hearts.

***Karma Yoga* Awareness:** The ONE's knowledge is like the sun bathing me and enveloping me in its warmth while I perform actions.

VARDATA: THE BESTOWER OF BLESSINGS

Introspection

The ONE speaks blessings not just through His lips but also from His heart.

Remembrance

Soul in Conversation with the ONE: My dear ONE, You have blessed me with a pure life, a life free of sorrow and anxiety, a life in which by nature I have generosity, a broad intellect, and an unlimited capacity for service. I have received these as a blessing and hence in all situations I experience full attainment.

The ONE in Conversation with the Soul: Sweet soul, like an innocent child, the innocent Lord, the ONE is easily pleased. Do you know the easiest way to please the Bestower of Blessings? Focus on the ONE, for that is what He loves the most. The souls who keep their promise to the ONE are themselves deeply loved by the Bestower of Blessings. Find strength in the ONE, find support in the ONE. Follow these instructions of the ONE and experience the sweetness of the ONE.

Practice

Soul Conscious *Drishti*: To constantly keep the ONE in my vision is to receive the greatest blessing from the ONE.

***Karma Yoga* Awareness:** The ONE gives a guaranteed blessing to the true servers: By your enthusiasm, that which you could not imagine will take place easily on the physical plane.

THE SUPREME BELOVED

Introspection

The more I love the ONE, the Beloved, the higher my happiness rises.

Remembrance

Soul in Conversation with the ONE: My dear ONE, the soul, know that my engagement with You is very powerful. You are the Beloved of all the epic love stories told over time. I sing love songs from my heart to You. Your gifts, as the Beloved's, last throughout eternity. All the celebrated love stories are the memorial of our love for each other at this time.

The ONE in Conversation with the Soul: Sweet soul, you know how to love, but now fulfill the responsibility of that love. Your spiritual Beloved is the Ocean of Love. The treasure store of love is overflowing. You are the light of My eyes, the jewel of My forehead, the necklace around My neck and the smile on My lips.

Practice

Soul Conscious *Drishti:* So intimate, so loving is my communication with the Beloved that we communicate with just a glance.

***Karma Yoga* Awareness:** As I go about my daily work, O Beloved, You appear before me. When I remember You, You come to me.

RUHANI SHAMA: THE SPIRITUAL FLAME

Introspection

The Spiritual Flame has come to awaken all human beings by igniting their inner lamp.

Remembrance

Soul in Conversation with the ONE: My dear ONE, You are the source of light of all who bring light to the world. You are a Spiritual Flame that always burns bright. You constantly serve others. At the festival of Diwali, the home is cleansed and a flame lit in every room. I clean the home of my heart and mind and invoke You.

The ONE in Conversation with the Soul: Sweet soul, you know that the light of your soul has dimmed. The ONE has now come to re-ignite your lamp. Your light is almost extinguished. I have especially come for you. Hence, sit and ignite your inner flame and the ONE will fill your heart and mind.

Practice

Soul Conscious *Drishti:* The smile on my lips and the light in my eyes reveal that I care, and that I share.

***Karma Yoga* Awareness:** I am a lamp that spreads Your light. I am a mirror that reflects Your light.

DHARAMRAJ: THE LORD OF RIGHTEOUSNESS

Introspection

The praise is of the ONE alone who puts right everything that has gone wrong.

Remembrance

Soul in Conversation with the ONE: My dear ONE, I understand that I am enjoying and suffering the just reactions to my own actions. I know a time will come when You will give me a clear vision of my unrighteous activity. So, I shouldn't hide anything from You; I shouldn't be too lenient with myself; and I shouldn't let the mirage deceive and seduce me. When I give in to this illusion, I punish myself by sabotaging my own happiness and power.

The ONE in Conversation with the Soul: Sweet soul, I will definitely tell you what is right. You are now becoming righteous. Righteous ones are those who take strength from the ONE. When you perform good actions, you receive good fruit of that. When you perform unrighteous actions you have to experience the consequence of that.

Practice

Soul Conscious *Drishti*: When my heart is clean, it unveils my vision and nothing false or degrading can blind me.

***Karma Yoga* Awareness:** I am clean inside and out. I realize the philosophy of karma and do service with honesty and lightness.

JEEVANMUKTI DATA: THE BESTOWER OF LIBERATION IN LIFE

Introspection

The ONE comes to give us freedom. That is why we call Him the Bestower of Liberation in Life.

Remembrance

Soul in Conversation with the ONE: My dear ONE, I want to fly, free as a bird. I cannot fly if I place myself in a golden or diamond cage. Desire for name and fame is my golden cage. The vanity of "I and mine" is my diamond cage.

The ONE in Conversation with the Soul: Sweet soul, the ONE continually teaches you how to be free. People say they want to free themselves from actions, but the ONE says: Pure actions will free you.

Practice

Soul Conscious *Drishti*: All souls are like kites and everyone's guiding kite string is in the ONE's hands. The ONE gives me the vision to fly in clear blue skies.

***Karma Yoga* Awareness:** I act purely when I help the ONE to open the gateway to my land of liberation in life, and to shut the gateway to my land of bondage.

RUDRA: THE ONE WHO CREATES THE SACRIFICIAL FIRE

Introspection

The ONE creates a cleansing fire in which we discard our sorrow and anxiety, so that we can attain peace and happiness.

Remembrance

Soul in Conversation with the ONE: My dear ONE, when You come, I will offer myself to You in love, because then You will offer Yourself to me in love. This is a pure exchange—I give myself to You and You give Yourself to me. How can I offer myself? How can I engage with integrity in this pure exchange?

The ONE in Conversation with the Soul: Sweet soul, you can give yourself fully by dedicating your intellect, reasoning and understanding to me and overcoming attachment to the illusion of body consciousness. Offer to Me all that you see with your body's eyes, including the body itself, and you will achieve self-sovereignty. I created this act of offering for your sovereignty.

Practice

Soul Conscious *Drishti:* I clearly see myself as a trustee. I responsibly manage my life on behalf of the ONE.

***Karma Yoga* Awareness:** I offer to the ONE the pure intentions of my mind, my body, and my wealth, and in return the ONE offers me self-sovereignty.

THE LORD OF THE POOR

Introspection

The ONE, the Lord of the Poor, wishes to bestow something by which everyone can become wealthy forever.

Remembrance

Soul in Conversation with the ONE: My dear ONE, many millionaires and billionaires in the world today give charity. Can You touch their heart and help them see the root of the world's problems, and not merely the symptoms? When it comes to material wealth, I have little to give. But I long to use all I have in Your task—please accept my pennies. Will the ONE inspire the wealthy to help with the real solution? How can I help this to happen?

The ONE in Conversation with the Soul: Sweet soul, I will accomplish My task bit by bit. I must create good fortune for many souls. It is not enough that ten or twenty souls use their vast resources in a worthwhile way. Many souls must dedicate all they have for the highest good. Sweet soul, whatever you have, dedicate all of it. Whatever you give from your heart, you will receive a thousand-fold in return. The ONE doesn't ask you for anything. He is the bestower by simply showing the way; He shows the poor how they can become wealthy.

Practice

Soul Conscious *Drishti*: I see the divine riches that the ONE is bestowing upon me.

***Karma Yoga* Awareness:** I remember – Mere drops of water can form a pure lake. With spiritual insight, I give my drops of righteous actions until they wash away my sorrow and poverty.

AKALMURAT: THE IMMORTAL IMAGE

Introspection

The ONE, the Image of Immortality, is the true *Satguru*.

Remembrance

Soul in Conversation with the ONE: My dear ONE, Your knowledge teaches me that I am an immortal soul present on the throne of the body. You have shown me that I am a tiny point of immortal light and hence indestructible. I, the soul, cannot die. I cannot be burned or buried like the body. Rituals are performed when my body dies.

The ONE in Conversation with the Soul: Sweet soul, I neither take birth nor die. I come only to liberate you from sorrow. You wouldn't say of the ONE that He died, or that He left His body. No rituals are performed when I leave because I do not have a mortal body. I am immortal, and in fact you are also immortal, but you come into the cycle of birth and death. I do not take birth through a womb. I do not become a human being. Ordinary souls have a physical image, but I am the immortal image.

Practice

Soul Conscious *Drishti*: In everyone I meet, I see an immortal soul sparkling on the throne of a body.

Karma Yoga **Awareness:** I remember the ONE who remains bodiless even as He inspires me to perform actions through my body.

SOMNATH: THE LORD OF NECTAR

Introspection

The ONE sprinkles nectar on me and even as I live, He makes my worries die in the burning flame of knowledge.

Remembrance

Soul in Conversation with the ONE: My dear ONE, You truly have revived me who had been a walking corpse. Now I understand why they say: The ONE brought the dead back to life. You have given me the nectar of spiritual knowledge and made me realize I am an immortal soul. I look at myself now and marvel at the transformation—someone whose life had no meaning is transformed into a special soul.

The ONE in Conversation with the Soul: Sweet soul, I am the very ONE to whom the whole world calls out. I belong to everyone. Everyone has a right to the ONE. The ONE loves the whole world. Now, know the ONE and love the ONE. Understand the ONE deeply as the Ocean of Knowledge and drink daily the nectar of knowledge I give you. This nectar of knowledge makes you immortal.

Practice

Soul Conscious *Drishti*: I see by the light of knowledge as I drink the nectar daily.

***Karma Yoga* Awareness:** I relish the nectar of knowledge and revive myself.

GOD OF THE DEVOTEES

Introspection

Devotees sing songs praising the ONE. However I never dreamed that He would sing songs praising me. I simply gave my heart to Him, but now He praises me.

Remembrance

Soul in Conversation with the ONE: My dear ONE, in the Copper and Iron Ages, I had changed everything into physical form, because I didn't have a divine intellect to discern the subtle significance. At this time, I appreciate the true devotees for their loving feelings and also because they remain single minded in any decision they make. I thank them from my heart for the memorials they have created of You. What is Your relationship with devotees?

The ONE in Conversation with the Soul: Sweet soul, the ONE also loves the devotees very much. Having heard the call of the devotees, I have now come. I come to give devotees the fruit of their devotion. My role starts in the Copper Age. Whatever devotional feelings you remember anyone with I fulfill those devotional feelings. I have no role in the Golden and Silver Ages. This is Drama. When the moment comes, the thought arises that I have to come. The ONE also thanks the devotees, because they have created auspicious occasions to spread enthusiasm and draw the attention of people to the ONE.

Practice

Soul Conscious *Drishti*: With divine insight, I now see what is reality and what is the memorial and stay in spiritual pleasure.

***Karma Yoga* Awareness:** With understanding and the right awareness, I forget the rituals of the path of devotion and remember my Home and the new world while performing actions.

SARVODAYA: THE ONE WHO HAS MERCY FOR ALL

Introspection

The ONE is the Liberator, the Merciful, and Blissful ONE.

Remembrance

Soul in Conversation with the ONE: My dear ONE, I was trapped in the prison of the five vices (*Ravan*). You had mercy on me and liberated Me. Your mercy is so all encompassing that You even elevated sinners like Ajamil and those weighed down by a stone-like intellect. Only You can have mercy on us!

The ONE in Conversation with the Soul: Sweet soul, because I have mercy for you, I come to make you virtuous. Constantly remember Me alone—this instruction is My mercy. You know that you cannot receive mercy from anyone other than the ONE. Even if the ONE empowers a special deity or elevated soul to be His instrument in rewarding your pure feelings, the ultimate Bestower is the ONE alone. My mercy has no limit.

Practice

Soul Conscious *Drishti:* Just as the ONE never loses hope even in those who seem hopeless, similarly, I maintain a vision of hope and mercy toward everyone.

***Karma Yoga* Awareness:** The Merciful ONE liberates me from the merciless one (*Ravan*).

SARVA-SHAKTIMAN: THE ONE WHO POSSESSES ALL POWERS

Introspection

The ONE is the Almighty Authority because He is 100% ever-pure.

Remembrance

Soul in Conversation with the ONE: My dear ONE, I stumbled from door to door along the pathways of life. I could never overcome the loneliness and emptiness I felt. I looked to people with occult powers to help me, but all I found in this world was darkness and heaviness. In the process, my head became dull, and my intellect turned to stone. This soul's battery gradually wore down. My dear ONE, show me Your power. Liberate me from *Maya*.

The ONE in Conversation with the Soul: Sweet soul, I now urge you to connect to Me (yoga), so that your battery fully charges with pure energy. By remembering Me, you will receive spiritual power. By connecting to Me, you receive abundant power and so become pure. The ONE grants you the right to all spiritual powers, for they are your birthright. You are My child and so I make you the master of all spiritual powers. From the movement of your birth, I bless you to attain all powers. My role is the greatest role of all; to transform the world by purifying the impure. My task is to change hell into heaven. Only the ONE has the power to purify souls of vice.

Practice

Soul Conscious *Drishti*: With my third eye, I see the ONE alone, the ONE who has no ego, despite His unlimited power.

***Karma Yoga* Awareness:** I take refuge in the all-powerful ONE. He truly has the power to attract me, so that I let go of all vices.

AMARNATH: THE LORD OF IMMORTALITY

Introspection

The eternal ONE comes and takes you, immortal souls, into the age of immortality, simply by telling you the story of immortality.

Remembrance

Soul in Conversation with the ONE: My dear ONE, I went through life as if blindly following a script. A deep weariness with the status quo set in. Then You came into my life and recounted the story of my immortality. You told me that I am a tiny imperishable soul and my imperishable role as soul continues eternally. You taught me to distinguish between illusion and reality. You told me the story of my past, present, and future and how the night of illusion is ending and the spiritual day is dawning.

The ONE in Conversation with the Soul: Sweet soul, I am the Lord of Immortality, and I tell you souls the true story of immortality, the story of your spiritual journey through time. Constantly remember Me alone and you will go to the land of immortality and your sins will be absolved. Always remember Me as I am and you will not suffer untimely death. I make you immortal. However, first you must love the ONE. If you get trapped in another body, you will fail to see the difference between the material world and the spiritual realm. Therefore, make your intellect very subtle and keep it beyond the illusions of this physical world.

Practice

Soul Conscious *Drishti*: : I gaze at the exquisite ONE, and I behold immortality within the ONE.

***Karma Yoga* Awareness:** Every day I listen to the story of immorality from the Lord of Immortality and I experience immortality.

THE BESTOWER OF LIBERATION

Introspection

The ONE who dwells in the sky calls out to those who dwell on earth: It is time to go Home.

Remembrance

Soul in Conversation with the ONE: My dear ONE, I was trapped and sinking in the quicksand of vices and was experiencing hell. Then I cried out to You to come and liberate me. You came and inspired me fully to renounce the vices. You inspired me to become indifferent to this dirty old world. You led me to spiritual study and promised to accompany me back to our real Home.

The ONE in Conversation with the Soul: Sweet soul, sever the knot that binds your intellect to this world. The cosmic play is now ending and you must go Home. I free you from the quicksand and take you back Home. To go back with Me, you must become a point of light. Your material life has spread like the branches of a tree, and to become a point of light, you must merge all of that tree back into its seed.

Practice

Soul Conscious *Drishti*: As I observe people, I envision them as a swarm of bees flying to their honeyed Home.

***Karma Yoga* Awareness:** I remember the ONE in our sweet Home. By such remembrance, I am able to return there.

THE OCEAN OF VIRTUES

Introspection

The ONE says: Oh souls, look within and see to what extent you have inculcated divine virtues.

Remembrance

Soul in Conversation with the ONE: My dear ONE, when I remember you as the Ocean of Virtues, I understand that kindness is more important than winning arguments. I invoke You when my mean-spiritedness tries to take over, for it will hurt me as much as the receiver. I must be honest with myself and recognize my own capacity to hurt other people. I must invoke You as the Ocean of Virtues. This invocation helps transform my nastiness into generosity.

The ONE in Conversation with the Soul: Sweet soul, treat everyone with love. I am the Ocean of Virtues and hence the Ocean of Happiness. I am making you like Me. The ONE is now filling you with this loving nature. I give you all My own virtues. Imbibe these divine virtues. Don't hurt anyone. The ONE's main virtue is to say to others, "You first." The ONE says: "Soul, you first!" Follow the ONE in this virtue.

Practice

Soul Conscious *Drishti*: The ONE makes me heir to His virtues. When I see this inheritance, I can then accept all those who are unkind to me.

***Karma Yoga* Awareness:** I constantly sing the ONE's praises in gratitude for all the benefits and virtues that I have received from the ONE.

THE WORLD BENEFACTOR

Introspection

The ONE takes on a great responsibility - to benefit the entire world.

Remembrance

Soul in Conversation with the ONE: My dear ONE, I love Your aspect as the World Benefactor. I love that Your one thought is: Let there be immediate benefit for all. I love that in Your words, there is always a variety of approaches for souls. I love that in Your eyes, there is always a searchlight to guide souls to their highest good. I love that You always remember Your benefactor helpers. Your every action is benevolent.

The ONE in Conversation with the Soul: Sweet soul, My vision is drawn to all the world's souls. I must give an inheritance to everyone. In My heart, I only remember that inheritance. As the ONE is praised as a world benefactor, so too are His children praised. And the children's form is like that of the ONE. As the ONE has all virtues, so do His children. And the ONE and His children share the same task.

Practice

Soul Conscious *Drishti*: The World Benefactor bestows, through my gaze, the stillness inherent in His being.

***Karma Yoga* Awareness:** I remember that the ONE, with my help, has come to fulfill His responsibility to the whole world.

THE INNOCENT LORD

Introspection

The ONE knocks on the door of my mind, offering me a palace for a pittance. Just see how much He gives me for all the insignificant old things that He takes!

Remembrance

Soul in Conversation with the ONE: My dear ONE, in the sublime early morning hours (*amrit vela*), I feel You most powerfully as the Innocent Lord. I feel so special because at that special time, You as the Innocent Lord fill the treasure chest of the soul. I experience love in all relationships as I celebrate a meeting with You. Our meeting at *amrit vela* is informal, endearing, and enriching. You have made an open offer to me to take whatever I desire. I must simply become Your child and take my due. Whatever I need, I come to You.

The ONE in Conversation with the Soul: Sweet soul, simply cherish this thought: "Whatever I am, I am yours." Come and sit down with Me, and dedicate your mind and intellect to Me. The ONE is the Friend, and He now offers you the throne of all rights. Make this bargain that endures life after life. Give Me all your old things, your worn baggage, and you will receive abundant new things in the Age of Truth, *Satyug*.

Practice

Soul Conscious *Drishti*: Just as the ONE honestly reveals who and what He is, so, too, I should honestly reveal myself to the ONE. With this clarity of vision, I elevate myself.

***Karma Yoga* Awareness:** The ONE taught me that the innocent are those of easy nature and pure feelings, clean and honest in mind and actions. Such innocent souls attract the ONE.

THE POWER PLANT

Introspection

I am constantly plugged into the Spiritual Power Plant. I am receiving light and strength from the ONE.

Remembrance

Soul in Conversation with the ONE: My dear ONE, Your spiritual current of light and power recharges my depleted self-respect. Your power transforms me forever. It shines a light on my blockages and bondages and destroys them. My constant connection to Your love and light gives me strength. This strength allows me to operate with equanimity and patience in this ever-changing world.

The ONE in Conversation with the Soul: Sweet soul, may you have an immortal spiritual life. You have a right to the light of My wisdom and the power that comes from being connected to Me. This right is your birthright as My precious child. Give yourself the happiness of existing as light. When you relish the joy of being light, you then draw upon My spiritual current. By receiving this power, you are easily transformed. The power that you experience will make you fearless, uninfluenced, and steadfast. Become a miniature powerhouse and be a conduit for this spiritual current.

Practice

Soul Conscious *Drishti*: I receive spiritual power from the ONE and gift that power through my eyes to everyone I meet.

***Karma Yoga* Awareness:** The energy I receive from being plugged into the ONE makes me sensible.

INSPERIENCE

THE DIAMOND SETTER

Introspection

You are the ONE who makes the world sparkle like a diamond, the ONE who makes matter sparkle like a diamond, the ONE who makes His children sparkle like precious diamonds.

Remembrance

Soul in Conversation with the ONE: My dear ONE, as a diamond setter delicately cuts a diamond, You fashion me with the blade of spiritual knowledge. You are a Diamond Merchant and each aspect of Your knowledge is an imperishable diamond. My value comes from recognizing the value of Your knowledge and remembering You constantly. Do You enjoy sorting us through Your fingers and setting us in jewelry that brings out the best of our color, facets, and sparkle?

The ONE in Conversation with the Soul: Sweet soul, the ONE always sees you in your complete brilliance. I see your unique and invaluable beauty. You are lucky, lovely, and loved. If you weighed the riches of the entire world on one scale and on the other scale the combined value of all of you precious diamonds, your value is far greater. Whether or not you see your own value, the ONE has seen the worthiness of each one of you. The ONE keeps valuable diamonds like you hidden away from *Maya*.

Practice

Soul Conscious *Drishti*: I see the soul, the diamond, sparkling in the center of each one's forehead.

Karma Yoga Awareness: I polish my rough edges and make myself a multi-faceted diamond on the field of service. I enter a close, sustained relationship with the Diamond Setter and become a special diamond.

TRIKALDARSHI: SEER OF THE THREE ASPECTS OF TIME

Introspection

By coming to know the ONE from the ONE, I understand the past, present, and the future.

Remembrance

Soul in Conversation with the ONE: My dear ONE, thank You for reassuring me about the future. Thank You for reviving my memories of the cosmic play's different phases. Thank You for making me strong and unshakeable. I went through life not knowing how my past affected my present and how my present affects my future. Even though You don't show me what will happen in the future, thank You for showing me how my present actions affect my future.

The ONE in Conversation with the Soul: Sweet soul, I come to share with you the secrets of the beginning, middle, and end of the cosmic play. You played a part but have forgotten. I see all your changes through time and have come to awaken your memories. By knowing this cosmic play entirely and the part you played in it, you will become its master. You must simply remember that you were once the most elevated of all human beings and you can become so again.

Practice

Soul Conscious *Drishti*: I watch the Drama as a witness and root myself in the eternal.

***Karma Yoga* Awareness:** I experience perfect stillness in the moment when I connect with the ONE who is the Seer of the three phases of time.

JAGANNATH: THE GUARDIAN OF THE UNIVERSE

Introspection

The whole world loves the ONE, because the ONE loves everyone in the world equally.

Remembrance

Soul in Conversation with the ONE: My dear ONE, You are always blissful and accessible. I am not afraid to approach You. When I come to You for shelter from the troubles of life, I never fear punishment or disapproval from You. You are always kind, generous, and reassuring. Even though You are the Guardian and Lord of the whole world, Your embrace feels comfortable, for coming to You, I have come home.

The ONE in Conversation with the Soul: Sweet soul, the entire world, at all times, belongs to the ONE. I am the Master of the entire world. I purify everyone. When you make My arms your home, then the entire world becomes your boundless home. Remember, life is a game, and those who play by the rules—by being loving and detached—win the game. Winning the game means to remember that no material thing ultimately belongs to you.

Practice

Soul Conscious *Drishti:* I become aware that the ONE is watching me with loving eyes as I act on the stage of the world.

***Karma Yoga* Awareness:** I take refuge with the ONE who is the protector and benefactor of the whole world.

THE SPIRITUAL SURGEON

Introspection

The ONE is the Supreme Laser Surgeon.

Remembrance

Soul in Conversation with the ONE: My dear ONE, You have access to the inner recesses of myself. Your cut is precise and painless. It feels like having laser surgery. You come into my deepest subconscious and vaporize my insecurities and weaknesses. Like a laser surgeon, You leave hardly a trace behind. You perform transformative surgery on the soul. I feel fresh and young in spirit after You've worked on me. What You do to my spirit is much more expansive and wondrous than anything an ordinary surgeon can do. Thank You for being my Spiritual Surgeon.

The ONE in Conversation with the Soul: Sweet soul, the ONE is the Surgeon of Eternal Truth. You become ever-healthy through the power of yoga. Only the ONE has the power to remove the alloy of vices from souls. I liberate you from all types of sorrow and illness. The five vices are the root cause of all ailments of the spirit. There is only one precaution you must take for post-operative care and for the surgery to work: fix your mind on Me.

Practice

Soul Conscious *Drishti*: I maintain a vision of compassion for other patients, knowing that they are going through a healing process.

***Karma Yoga* Awareness:** I keep my spirit light and open for the Eternal Surgeon to come and work on me.

TRILOKINATH: LORD OF THE THREE WORLDS

Introspection

The ONE rejuvenates me with a grand tour of the material world, the subtle angelic world, and the eternal Home.

Remembrance

Soul in Conversation with the ONE: My dear ONE, You expertly create the Golden Age, yet You have no personal need for a material body or material experience. You know the subtle angelic world perfectly where a mere glance or gesture communicates all, for You create that world as well. You are the perfect Master of the eternal Home because, even there, You are free and unattached. Most amazing of all is the ease with which You move between the three worlds.

The ONE in Conversation with the Soul: Sweet soul, now understand the subtle angelic world and the eternal Home. Go to both worlds and learn to be still in a second within each by fully stopping the past. Create an inner sanctuary—this will empower you to be a master of the three worlds. I leave My throne in the eternal Home to come and teach you this. The eternal Home is your throne too, for you are a soul.

Practice

Soul Conscious *Drishti:* I can't take my eyes off the Resident of the far away land Who comes to meet me.

***Karma Yoga* Awareness:** : I become comfortable in my own skin while remembering the ONE in the eternal Home.

THE CREATOR

Introspection

I reflect on the One's gift to me of a living temple.

Remembrance

Soul in Conversation with the ONE: My dear ONE, You seem to be constructing a beautiful temple—a living ode to peace, ecstasy, and prosperity. Sometimes I wonder why certain situations happen in my life or certain people come and go, until I realize that they are but bricks in the temple. The combinations of my thoughts, words, actions, relationships, and connections all help quietly to place brick after brick in this temple. Some might be discarded because they are not fully baked or perfect, but ultimately Your silent hand moves the whole process.

The ONE in Conversation with the Soul: Sweet soul, I have come to establish the Golden Age of humanity. I have come to make you worthy of living there. The ONE is called the eternal Creator. All others are the creation. The creation bestows no inheritance to anyone. Only I grant you your inheritance. The creation should remember the Creator. I transform the world and make it new. This is the working out of the cosmic play. I bring heaven on the palm of My hand for you children. The sign of My love is that I give you all you need to become complete.

Practice

Soul Conscious *Drishti:* I see the beauty of the Creator in His creation.

***Karma Yoga* Awareness:** The ONE is helping me create my reward by transforming my actions.

THE ALTRUISTIC ONE

Introspection

The ONE is egoless, humble, and altruistic.

Remembrance

Soul in Conversation with the ONE: My dear ONE, You are so altruistic because You are pure. You are so beautiful because You are selfless. I can't stop marveling at Your supreme altruism and Your unlimited, pure concern for my well-being. Your one desire is to selflessly serve us souls. You expect no compensation or benefit when You serve. Your devotion to, and regard for, my welfare creates a longing in me to please You. How can I reciprocate Your tireless, selfless service?

The ONE in Conversation with the Soul: Sweet soul, just as I become a Tireless Server, so you should also be a tireless server. I am pleased with those who serve well. I teach you spiritual service. Learn to serve souls because through this service there is real lasting benefit. Just as I am an ever ignited lamp that spiritually awakens everyone in the world, you, too, must perform this wonderful service. Don't pursue limited gain and glory. I will give you an unlimited reward for your altruistic, selfless service.

Practice

Soul Conscious *Drishti*: I keep my eye on the intrinsic reward received from selfless service and do not pursue temporary gain.

***Karma Yoga* Awareness:** I take every opportunity to serve selflessly for the welfare of everyone.

THE BESTOWER OF DIVINE WISDOM

Introspection

The ONE has come to the door of my awareness to unlock my wisdom.

Remembrance

Soul in Conversation with the ONE: My dear ONE, Your divine wisdom is a goddess that speaks to me. More than just speaking, she sings to me — moving melodies, carried on a cosmic breeze from Your heart to mine. She awakens me. She weaves songs of inspiration and enthusiasm till I open my third eye. I must awake and seize the day.

The ONE in Conversation with the Soul: Sweet soul, as soon as you wake, the first words that should emerge from your lips are: "My beloved ONE." I bestowed divine wisdom on you by which you know yourself as soul and remember Me as I am in My original form. You must love Me alone. While seeing a body, remember Me. You received the third eye in order to see Me and understand Me. Make use of it. Divine wisdom is the key that opens an unlimited treasure chest. Play with the wisdom jewels in the treasure chest and ignore the baubles of the material world.

Practice

Soul Conscious *Drishti*: Through my third eye, I see the value of every soul and the beauty of every moment.

***Karma Yoga* Awareness:** I maintain courage and perform pure actions so the lock to the treasure chest stays open.

SATGURU: THE TRUE GURU

Introspection

The *Satguru* showers me with the light of knowledge, dispelling the darkness of my ignorance.

Remembrance

Soul in Conversation with the ONE: My dear ONE, You show me the path Home and accompany me on the return journey Home. Your Home is my Home. I'm trapped in the maze of the body and bodily relationships. You guide me out of the maze to the gates of the Golden Age. With You as my Guru, I can pass the most difficult obstacle course (difficult relationships and situations) and emerge fresh and eager for the next stage of my journey. You show me a path, where I saw a wall. I'm so fortunate to have You as my Guru.

The ONE in Conversation with the Soul: Sweet soul, the destination you reach depends on the directions you follow. Your real destination is peace and happiness. Don't forget this real destination and get lost in a false destination (name, fame, and material gain). Detach your heart from the material world, root your understanding in your true identity as a soul beyond the body, and be always aware of your Home. When you follow these directions, you not only reach your real destination, but also receive blessings from the *Satguru*, the true Guru.

Practice

Soul Conscious *Drishti:* When I am in the company of the ONE, my eyes radiate the light that connects other souls to the ONE companion.

***Karma Yoga* Awareness:** On performing an action, I bring my thoughts to its essence. I merge all diffused impressions into one point of experience.

THE DESTROYER OF OBSTACLES

Introspection

Success is where the ONE is.

Remembrance

Soul in Conversation with the ONE: My dear ONE, to experience You as a Destroyer of Obstacles, I must see those obstacles as blessings. When I see obstacles as gifts and take time to unwrap them and perceive the learning inherent in them, then You show me the way to overcome them. I successfully master them only when I remember You from my heart. Actually, when I keep Your company, I feel I can fly over all obstacles.

The ONE in Conversation with the Soul: Sweet soul, just be aware that, "I am detached and loved by the ONE, and so the whole burden belongs to Him." When you know this, then in the love of the Destroyer of Obstacles, what problem can arise? I understand the problem and am responsible for it. When you become light in this way, everything else also becomes light. Make all relationships with Me. When all relationships are right, the problems finish. Keep the soul constantly cheerful. When you do this, I will take responsibility to keep *Maya's* attractions away from you. The ONE gives you this special guarantee.

Practice

Soul Conscious *Drishti:* I transform my perception of barriers and look at them as blessings.

***Karma Yoga* Awareness:** I keep myself cheerful and remember the ONE's guarantee to me.

YOGESHWARA: THE LORD OF YOGA

Introspection

The ONE teaches me true yoga and that is why He is *Yogeshwar*.

Remembrance

Soul in Conversation with the ONE: My dear ONE, You give me the great mantra of "*manmanabhav*" (focus of the mind on the ONE). This spiritual practice links You and me. You yoke my mind to You and harness my heart to Yours. You show me that, with the power of concentration, I restore myself to my original beauty and brilliance, and sustain my connection with You. Thank You for teaching me how to remember my pure self and unite with You.

The ONE in Conversation with the Soul: Sweet soul, I am the ONE Who kindles your light through yoga, the ONE Who satisfies your hunger, and the ONE Who removes all your sickness. I remember you more than you remember Me. I chant your good qualities like a mantra. Even though you may forget Me, I will always remember you. I have no other business than to remember you.

Practice

Soul Conscious *Drishti:* I have a pure wish and vision for every soul I meet today, and that links me to the ONE.

***Karma Yoga* Awareness:** I maintain the sparkle of an easy yogi's life as I work, walk, and move around.

THE TEACHER

Introspection

The ONE teaches, "Consider yourself to be a soul and remember Me."

Remembrance

Soul in Conversation with the ONE: My dear ONE, I first experienced You as my Teacher. You taught me how to be a child. You taught me how to be your friend. And most importantly, you taught me to be spiritually mature and carry my weight. You reformed and refined me. You teach with such humility and love. Show me how to teach others to love You.

The ONE in Conversation with the Soul: Sweet soul, when you teach spiritual knowledge, but focus on the body, the student soul doesn't listen. Now become soul conscious. *Maya* has extinguished your lamp. I pour the oil of spiritual knowledge into you, the soul, and reignite your lamp. I am, by nature, the Teacher. I explain the secrets of the Creator and creation to you. I love everyone and will always love everyone. These teachings express My love. Day and night, the ONE only thinks of how to educate you so that you progress. You reach the highest destination when you do not remember anyone else, and by such exclusive remembrance of Me, you break all body consciousness. So great is this test, that I personally come to teach you!

Practice

Soul Conscious *Drishti:* I see the value of the teachings and study with sincerity and dedication.

***Karma Yoga* Awareness:** I learn the art of silence while operating in the world of sound.

THE BUSINESSMAN

Introspection

The ONE is the greatest Businessman. Just see what He takes from me and what He gives me in return.

Remembrance

Soul in Conversation with the ONE: My dear ONE, I like doing business with You. Your business is both a divine retail store and an investment firm. You give the highest rate of return on any investment I make with You. Some investments can be put off, some might have better outcomes if left alone for a while. But when dealing with You, I cannot afford to procrastinate. This is something I must do right here and right now. I implicitly and explicitly trust You as a Businessman and I trust Your sense of timing. What does Your retail store offer?

The ONE in Conversation with the Soul: Sweet soul, yes, I deal in divine merchandise such as peace, purity, freedom, wisdom, bliss, and all kinds of happiness. There cannot be any happiness greater than making a deal with Me. Anyone can come and do business with Me. In My divine retail store, nothing is unattained. However, many don't understand how to deal with Me. While taking, they tire. You must give Me all your old things (old patterns of thinking and doing) and trade them for new. I give many millions of times what you give Me. I do this business and you must do it, too.

Practice

Soul Conscious *Drishti*: I see beneath the surface of what seems a simple transaction with the ONE. I see the hidden layer of wisdom that puts vital processes in motion to make real spiritual progress.

***Karma Yoga* Awareness:** The ONE, the Businessman, knows how to keep a good account of profit and loss. He teaches me to go from loss to profit.

THE SERVER

Introspection

Do I know what the ONE's life is all about? Service is the cornerstone of the ONE's life.

Remembrance

Soul in Conversation with the ONE: My dear ONE, You come and do the most elevated service for me. You transform me, a pauper, into a spiritual prince. Whatever quality I lack, You bring to me. But I must be honest with You. You fulfill the shortcoming in my spirit so quietly, drawing no attention to Yourself, nor taking credit. As You are humble in serving Me, I must be humble in serving You.

The ONE in Conversation with the Soul: Sweet soul, I am egoless and eager to serve you. I am here to fulfill your spiritual needs such as perseverance, self-mastery, empathy, and charity—whenever and however you seek them, and for whatever reason. Just as servers are summoned with one word, you can summon Me with one pure act of surrender to Me. The ONE is loving and obedient to those who surrender themselves to Him. I stand before you as Your Humble Server to help you. Use Me!

Practice

Soul Conscious *Drishti*: I visualize the ONE helping me with a thousand arms.

***Karma Yoga* Awareness:** I take one step of courage in return for a thousand-fold help from the ONE, my Server.

THE DIRECTOR AND PRODUCER

Introspection

The ONE directs and produces the grand epic Movie of all that is life.

Remembrance

Soul in Conversation with the ONE: My dear ONE, I want You to direct my acting. I want to take my cues from You and not from the other actors in the grand epic Movie playing on the world stage. You have a broad, unlimited vision of what must happen for the Movie to have a happy ending. I must remember: You choose the other cast members. Their script is not in my hands. I want to help You realize Your complete vision for the grand epic Movie.

The ONE in Conversation with the Soul: Sweet soul, O soul, do you recognize Me? I am the Creator, Director and Producer of the unlimited Drama. I have created a Drama for happiness, not sorrow. You are an imperishable soul and your role continues eternally. I, too, have a part in the grand epic Movie. I come to make old, impure souls new. I come at My precise time, according to the Drama's plan, and take you back Home. I, too, play an eternal, imperishable part within the Drama.

Practice

Soul Conscious *Drishti:* I watch the Movie as a witness. I have the best seat in the theater, for the ONE, the Director and Producer, is my loving Parent and He belongs to me.

***Karma Yoga* Awareness:** With the ONE, I go on a grand spiritual adventure filled with romance and drama.

The Brahma Kumaris present a unique spiritual understanding of the ONE. These sacred teachings were originally given to the world in Hindi, whose roots lie in the Sanskrit language of India. Some Sanskrit terms, such as yoga, guru, and karma, are already common English words. We decided to retain a few other key terms, with clear translations, to give the reader an authentic taste of that celebrated spiritual tradition.

Abhogata	One who is beyond physical experiences such as taste and smell.
Asochata	One who is beyond worries.
Ajamil	An innocent brahmin youth who fell into decadence, only to be saved at the end by the ONE's mercy.
Amarnath	Immortal Lord. A famous pilgrimage place and a temple to the ONE.
Amrit	Nectar.
Amrit Vela	Vela means time. Hence, a time for receiving nectar. It falls between 2am and 5:00am in the early morning hours.
Atma	Soul.
Bhatti	A period of powerful yoga, literally a fireplace or oven.
Bholanath	Lord of the Innocent Ones.
Body Consciousness	Thinking the temporary body is the real self.
Buddhi	Wisdom, understanding, reasoning, awareness, intellect.
Confluence Age	It is the meeting of two ages, namely the Iron Age and the Golden Age. It is when the night of ignorance ends and the day of enlightenment begins.
Copper Age	Age in which the human soul is reactive to being in the body and begins to experience low-grade forms of the vices such as lust, anger, greed, ego and attachment.

Glossary of Terms

Dipawali/Diwali	Literally "rows of lamps," a Hindu festival of lights celebrated in the autumn.
Dipak	An earthenware lamp.
Drama	The theatrics of life, the cosmic "movie."
Drishti	Seeing, viewing, and beholding with the mind's eye.
Golden Age	An age of beauty and harmony on earth. All souls will be in their highest stage of purity and perfection.
Iron Age	Age of total body consciousness. In this age ignorance rules and souls experience sorrow. In this age the world reaches its most degraded stage.
Jadugar	Magician. Jadu = magic.
Kalpa	An eon, a vast period of time, and by extension the myriad generations that appear during this time.
Karankaravanhar	The ONE who works directly and also works through others.
Karma	Literally means action. Action that produces worldly reaction, the cause and effect of destiny.
Karmateet	One who has gone beyond the effects of karma.
Karma Yoga	Action performed while in a state of being connected to the ONE. Connecting to the ONE through our work in the world.
Khuda	A name for the ONE, used by Muslims.
Manmanabhav	Literally means, "Fix your mind on me." An instruction of the ONE.
Mansa Seva	Mansa is mind and seva is service. Serving with the mind.
Maya	The supernatural power of illusion. Human weaknesses. A product of body consciousness and the five vices such as lust, anger, greed, ego, and attachment.

Mukti	A state of perfect peace and liberation that human souls experience in the Home of souls.
Pandavas	The five sons of King Pandu, heroes of the Mahabharat war – Yudhishthira, Bhima, Arjuna, Nakula and Sahadeva.
Paramdham	The supreme abode, home of human souls and of the ONE.
Ravan	An ancient demon whose name comes to symbolize extreme vice.
Ravan Rajya	The kingdom of ravan, i.e. a place where vices rule.
Saligrams	In some parts of India, a round stone or dough object representing the soul in physical form.
Satya/Sat	Truth.
Satyuga	The age of truth, considered the Golden Age of humanity.
Shivalingam	A stone representation of Shiva as a manifestation of God.
Somnath	Lord of Nectar. One of the first temples built to the ONE.
Soul Consciousness	When human beings are in a state of original awareness of being spirit. When each thought and action is imbued with love, peace, wisdom, purity, and bliss.
Shivam	The benevolent ONE.
Silver Age	Age where souls begin to slightly lose their perfection. It is a reflection of the Golden Age. Still a joyful world and souls are still experiencing liberation-in-life.
Sundaram	The beautiful ONE.
Swadharma	Swa is "one's own" and dharma is sacred duty. Swadharma is the original duty of the soul.
Vikarmajit	One who has conquered negative karma.
Yoga	Connection of the human soul with ONE, the Supreme Soul.

85

Gayatri Naraine is a fascinating speaker, writer, and educator whose love for truth and God touch the heart and carry the intellect to new heights. Since 1980, she has been the representative of the Brahma Kumaris to the United Nations in New York. She currently serves on the board of directors of Images and Voices of Hope and is also part of the design team for the Call-of-the-Time Dialogues. Gayatri has co-authored a number of publications and books, the most recent books include: *The Story of Immortality: A Return to Self Sovereignty* and *Something Beyond Greatness: Conversations with a Man of Science and a Woman of God*. Gayatri was born in Guyana and currently lives in New York City, USA.

Shireen Chada has studied, practiced, and taught spiritual meditation for twenty years. She is the author of a book [*True Hollywood Blockbuster: The Making of Divine Heroes*], two popular meditation CDs [*The 8 Spiritual Powers* and *Real Reflections*], and a deck of spiritual power cards [*The 8 Spiritual Powers*]. Shireen has designed and facilitated retreats and workshops to assist participants more easily to embrace the perennial wisdom presented in her books and CDs. She is also the presenter on the *Release Your Wings* TV Show (www.releaseyourwings.net). She leads the Brahma Kumaris Meditation Center of Tampa Bay, Florida. Shireen's effective and insightful techniques for spiritual transformation powerfully uplift the soul.